# The Spy Who Came In For The Phone

A comedy
Alan Richardson

**New Theatre Publications - London**
www.plays4theatre.com

**2**

© 2013 BY Alan Richardson
First published in 2004

The edition published in 2013

New Theatre Publications

2 Hereford Close | Warrington | Cheshire | WA1 4HR | 01925 485605

www.plays4theatre.com    email: info@plays4theatre.com

New Theatre Publications is the trading name of the publishing house that is owned by members of the Playwrights' Co-operative. This innovative project was launched on the 1st October 1997 by writers Paul Beard and Ian Hornby with the aim of encouraging the writing and promotion of the very best in New Theatre by Professional and Amateur writers for the Professional and Amateur Theatre at home and abroad.

ISBN 9 781 840 94926 1

**Characters**

**Ron**
**Mrs Davies**
**Chris Taylor**
**Sally Taylor**
**Ludmila**
**P.C. Nash**

4

## Copyright Information

The play is fully protected under the Copyright laws of the British Commonwealth of Nations, the United States of America and all countries of the Berne and Universal Copyright Conventions.

All rights including Stage, Motion Picture, Radio, television, Public Reading, and Translation into Foreign Languages, are strictly reserved.

No part of this publication may lawfully be reproduced in ANY form or by any means - photocopying, typescript, recording (including video-recording), manuscript, electronic, mechanical or otherwise - or be transmitted or stored in a retrieval system, without prior permission.

Licenses for amateur performances are issued subject to the understanding that it shall be made clear in all advertising matter that the audience will witness an amateur performance; that the names of the authors of the plays shall be included on all programmes, and that the integrity of the authors' work will be preserved.

The Royalty Fee is subject to contract and subject to variation at the sole discretion of New Theatre Publications.

In Theatres of Halls seating Four Hundred or more the fee will be subject to negotiation.

In Territories Overseas the fee quoted may not apply. A fee will be quoted on application to New Theatre Publications, London.

## Video-Recording of Amateur Productions

Please note that the copyright laws governing video-recording are extremely complex and that it should not be assumed that any play may be video-recorded for whatever purpose without first obtaining the permission of the appropriate agents. The fact that a play is published by New Theatre Publications does not indicate that video rights are available or that New Theatre Publications control such rights.

## Performing Licence Applications

A performing licence for these plays will be issued by "New Theatre Publications" subject to the following conditions.

### Conditions

1. That the performance fee is paid in full on the date of application for a licence.

2. That the name of the author(s) is/are clearly shown in any programme or publicity material.

3. That the author(s) is/are entitled to receive two complimentary tickets to see his/her/their work in performance if they so wish.

4. That a copy of the play is purchased from New Theatre Publications for each named speaking part and a minimum of three copies purchased for backstage use.

5. That a copy of any review be forwarded to New Theatre Publications.

6. That the New Theatre Publications logo is clearly shown on any publicity material. This is available on our website.

### Fees

Details of script prices and fees payable for each performance or public reading can be obtained by telephone to (+44) 01925 485605 or to the address below.

Alternatively, latest prices can be obtained from our website www.plays4theatre.com where credit/debit cards can be used for payment.

To apply for a performing licence for any play please write to New Theatre Publications 2 Hereford Close, Warrington, Cheshire WA1 4HR or email info@plays4theatre.com with the following details:-

1. Name and address of theatre company.

2. Details of venue including seating capacity.

3. Dates of proposed performance or public reading.

4. Contact telephone number for Author's complimentary tickets.

Or apply directly via our website at www.plays4theatre.com

## The Spy Who Came in for the Phone
### a one act comedy by Alan Richardson
*cast (in order of appearance)*

**Ron** *a telephone engineer, forties or older*
**Mrs Davies** - *a friendly neighbour, forties or older*
**Chris Taylor** - *new occupant of the flat, late teens, twenties or thirties*
**Sally Taylor** - *his wife, aged to match Chris*
**Ludmila** - *an unexpected female visitor – either glamorously young or seductively mature*
**P.C. Nash** - *male or female, any age*

**Time**   *Late 1960's*
**Setting**   *The living room of an unfurnished flat.*
*There is one entrance leading to a hall and an outside door. A window overlooks the street below. The walls show evidence of an attempt to decorate, with stripped wallpaper and/or trial patches of different paints. A stepladder, tins of paints, and other decorating-soon-to-begin items are scattered about.*
*The only item of furniture is a paint-splattered wooden chair.*
*Occupying this chair is Ron, a telephone engineer. Ron is very busy - reading a newspaper and drinking tea. Beside him are his toolbox, a small open cardboard box and a clipboard with a large number of official forms. A telephone cable, running from a wall socket, lies unconnected. He also has a sixties style transistor radio which is playing loudly. (Suggested music - anything from an early James Bond film)*
*We hear a door opened and closed offstage. Ron is unconcerned and continues to read his newspaper. Mrs Davies enters. She is your "friendly neighbour" that no block of flats could be without, although she is less than friendly at the sight of the non-working Ron.*

**Mrs D**   Are you still here?
**Ron**   Looks like it, doesn't it?
**Mrs D**   And you're not finished yet?
**Ron**   Don't look like it, does it?
**Mrs D**   *(struggling to hear above the radio.)* What was that?
**Ron**   What was what?
**Mrs D**   What? *(Pointing to the radio.)* Do you mind?
**Ron**   What?
**Mrs D**   The radio!
**Ron**   Oh... right! *(He switches it off.)*

**Mrs D**    Thank you. That's better. I don't know how you can work in that racket. Perhaps explains why you haven't been working, as far I can see.

**Ron**    *(reluctantly putting aside his newspaper.)* I'll have you know I've been very busy, Mrs... sorry, I've forgotten. *(He gets up.)*

**Mrs D**    Davies.

**Ron**    Mrs Davies. *(He hands her his cup.)* Thanks. I wouldn't say no to a refill.

**Mrs D**    That'll be your third. How many cups of tea, and hours, does it take to install a phone?

**Ron**    This isn't one of your slap-dash jobs. Connecting a telephonic apparatus requires an expertly trained technician.

**Mrs D**    Does it? So when are the GPO sending one?

**Ron**    Ha-ha. I'll have you know you were lucky to get me.

**Mrs D**    It's the nice young couple who bought this flat who were lucky, not me. I only have their keys to admit tradesmen. They didn't say they were expecting a telephone engineer, so you were lucky to catch me on the stairs.

**Ron**    And they were lucky they didn't find an LZ203 behind their door.

**Mrs D**    A what?

**Ron**    An LZ203. *(He produces his clipboard and selects a form.)* Cancellation of a scheduled installation due to inability to gain access to domestic property. A proper form for every task. That's what I like to see. Do you know what makes Britain great? It's not your Beatles or Carnaby Street. It's paperwork, meticulously prepared and correctly completed. I've got an official GPO form for every contingency you'd care to mention.

**Mrs D**    I don't think I care to, thank you.

**Ron**    Believe me, you don't want to find an LZ203 behind your door.

**Mrs D**    That wouldn't bother me. I don't have a telephone.

**Ron**    But we're living in nineteen-sixties. How can you manage without a phone?

**Mrs D**    Very easily. The only person I phone is my sister in Ipswich. When I need to call her, I use the phone box at the corner of the street. I keep telling her to do the same. Especially since she started getting strange calls.

**Ron**    *(very interested)* Does she now?

**Mrs D**    Some man keeps phoning her asking some very odd questions.

**Ron**    What sort of questions? I'm only enquiring in an official capacity.

**Mrs D**  You wouldn't believe the things he comes out with.

**Ron**  Like?

**Mrs D**  You know... Well, the other night, just about midnight, he phones and asks her what she's wearing underneath her...

**Ron**  Yes?

**Mrs D**  None of your nosy business! Kindly get on with whatever you're supposed to be doing.

**Ron**  An LZ920d. Standard installation of telephonic apparatus within a domestic property. Not to be confused with an LZ920c. That's installation within a commercial property.

**Mrs D**  Whatever "LZ" it is, kindly start "LZ"ing. I don't mind being an obliging neighbour, up to a point, which you passed ages ago.

**Ron**  Won't be much longer. Here we are... *(Ron produces a bright red telephone with an old-style dial from the cardboard box.)* One model twelve.

**Mrs D**  It's a bit loud.

**Ron**  How do you know? You haven't heard it ring yet. Oh, you mean the colour? Yes. But you should see some of the phones I install. *(He begins connecting the wires.)* This is a very nice flat.

**Mrs D**  It will be... once it's properly decorated.

**Ron**  A flat here in Kensington must cost a packet. House prices are getting ridiculous. My manager just bought a house in Victoria. Do you know what he paid, just to live in the middle of London? Seven thousand pounds! Crazy! *(Ron is getting tangled in the various trailing cables.)* You know, I dream of the day we'll have phones without all the cords and cables. But it'll never happen. Technically, it can't be done.

**Mrs D**  Are you sure you know what you're doing?

**Ron**  Of course! I'll have you know, I'm well trained.

**Mrs D**  So's my cocker spaniel. But he doesn't take two hours to go for a....

**Ron**  All right. That's it done. I just need to make sure we're connected to the exchange.

*(Noises off. A male voice is heard.)*

**Chris**  *(off)* Hello? Is that you, Mrs D?

**Mrs D**  Yes. Through here.

*(Chris and Sally enter. They are young recently-weds. He is carrying tins of paint. She is carrying rolls of wallpaper. They leave everything on the floor and drape their coats over the*

*stepladder.)*

**Sally** Hello, Mrs Davies. We're in your debt again.

**Mrs D** Don't mention it.

**Chris** Thanks again. We really must get a spare set of keys cut.

**Mrs D** *(reluctantly surrendering their keys.)* You should. But I must be on my way.

**Sally** Of course. Don't let us hold you back.

**Mrs D** I'm just across the landing if you need me. In fact, how about a nice cuppa before you start work?

**Ron** *(presenting his cup.)* Thanks. Thought you'd never ask.

**Mrs D** The offer is for Mr and Mrs Taylor. *(Snatches his cup.)* You've already had two too many.

**Chris** Yes, I was about to ask. Who's this?

**Ron** Ron. Nice to meet you.

**Sally** Likewise. I'm Sally. My husband, Chris.

**Chris** I don't think we've met before.

**Ron** GPO telephone engineer.

**Mrs D** And he's been here for three hours.

**Sally** Doing what?

**Mrs D** Apart from two cups of tea and reading a newspaper, not very much. I'll leave you to sort him out. Be back with your tea in two ticks. *(Exits.)*

**Sally** Thanks, Mrs Davies.

**Ron** Right. I've tested your line and everything's... as you younger generation say... groovy.
*(Chris and Sally exchange a look.)*
You don't realise how lucky you are.

**Chris** Are we? Fancy that.

**Ron** Not only did you get an LZ920d; standard installation within a domestic property, but somehow, you managed to get a 920d*p*.

**Chris** Did we? Well, what can we say except... what's the "p" for?

**Ron** Priority Installation. Don't know how you managed to pull that one.

**Chris** Beats us too. Especially when...

**Ron** So all that's left is your LZ406 acknowledging delivery and installation of your telephonic apparatus. *(He produces the said form from his clipboard.)* Don't forget to complete both sides, and sign here... here... and date and sign here.

**Chris** Yes, very nice. But I'm afraid we have a slight problem here.

**Ron** A problem? *(This is a word Ron doesn't like to encounter.)*

| | |
|---|---|
| Chris | It's not that we're complaining. On the contrary, we're impressed. *(To Sally)* Aren't we? |
| Sally | Oh, yes. Such a marvellous service. Our very own phone. Personally delivered and installed. |
| Chris | *Priority* installed. Which is really something. Especially when we didn't order one. |
| Ron | *(not wanting to hear this.)* You didn't order this phone? |
| Chris | Definitely not. |
| Sally | Especially *that* colour. We do need a phone, but we haven't actually ordered one yet. |
| Ron | But you must have ordered this phone. |
| Chris | No. I think there's been a mistake. |
| Ron | A mistake? *(Another word he doesn't like to hear.)* Impossible. *(He searches his clipboard.)* I must have your LZ702 somewhere. That's the form requesting installation. Somebody here signed it. |
| Chris | Not us. It's obviously someone else's phone. |
| Ron | Can't be. That never happens when I'm on the job. |
| Sally | Hang on, Chris. We are going to get a phone, eventually. Why not have this one? |
| Ron | Yes. Good idea. |
| Chris | *(to Ron)* Do you mind? *(To Sally)* We could... but I don't fancy having someone else's phone. |
| Sally | It'll save time. No waiting for another engineer. |
| Chris | You've got a point. But I'd still prefer our own choice of phone. |
| Sally | This one's beginning to grow on me. |
| Ron | Mr Taylor, could you decide, please? |
| Chris | It's not for me to decide. |
| Sally | We make joint decisions. We have a modern marriage. |
| Ron | I see. One of them women's libbers. So what's the joint decision? |
| Chris | *(to Sally)* We keep it? |
| Sally | We keep it. *(To Ron)* On one condition? No more forms. |
| Ron | If you're keeping it, your existing LZ920dp will do. |
| Chris | Great. So that's us all connected? |
| Ron | Yes. Everything's swinging. |
| Sally | Wonderful. *(She steers him towards the door.)* It's been a pleasure... of sorts. |
| Chris | *(presenting Ron with his clipboard, toolbox and newspaper.)* But we've got loads to do. |

**Ron**      Yes, but I'm sure I've forgotten something.

**Chris/Sally** Goodbye!

*(They almost push him out. But in an instant, he is back.).*

**Chris/Sally** Yes?

**Ron**      You do want your new number? *(He consults his paperwork.)*

**Chris**    Yes. It would be handy to know.

**Sally**    Our first phone number as man and wife. Isn't it romantic? *(She snuggles up to him.)*

**Chris**    *(responding)* If you insist.

**Ron**      Excuse me? Thank you. Your number is Kensington 1-9-1-7.

**Sally**    Hang on 'till I write it down. *(She finds a notepad in her bag.)* I'll never remember that. "K-e-n 1-9-1-7". Why do they make phone numbers so big?

**Ron**      *(eager to explain)* Well, there's a number of reasons. First of all...

**Chris**    Yes! Thank you! Goodbye!

*(They get him out again.)*

**Sally**    Are we expecting anyone else? Plumbers? Electricians? Exorcists?

**Chris**    No. But we weren't expecting him.

**Sally**    At least we've seen the last of him. And we've got our new phone. *(She picks it up and thinks about where to place it.)* I wonder where it should go? How about here? *(She places it on the chair, and then finds a more suitable position for the chair.)* Although this does mean we'll need to rethink our colour scheme for this room.

**Chris**    Why?

**Sally**    A bright red phone's going to clash horribly with the colour we had in mind.

**Chris**    Does that matter?

**Sally**    Does that... Honestly! Men! Next question; who'll be the first person to phone us?

**Chris**    That's an easy one. Your mother. *(The phone rings.)* Talk of the devil. Go on then?

**Sally**    No, you answer it.

**Chris**    That doesn't sound like a true women's libber.

**Sally**    Please?

**Chris**    OK. *(He picks up the phone.)* Hello... Kensington... *(He checks the notepad.)* 1-9-1-7. What...? What...? Say that again? Yes, but I don't understand... Who's calling? Hello? Hello? *(He* *replaces the phone.)* Gone.

**Sally**   Well?

**Chris**   It was a message. A very strange message. You're not going to believe it.

**Sally**   Try me.

**Chris**   "The yellow zebra is leaving Vienna on the midnight train".

**Sally**   You're right. I don't believe it. That doesn't sound like mum.

**Chris**   Definitely not. A male voice. Heavy accent. Sort of middle European.

**Sally**   "The yellow zebra is leaving Vienna on the midnight train". But that's silly.

**Chris**   Completely. Everybody knows zebras are black and white.

**Sally**   Wrong number? Or a hoax? Has to be.

**Chris**   Possibly. But this phone has just been connected. No one else knows our number. *(The phone rings again.)* OK. Your turn this time.

**Sally**   Right. *(She picks up the phone.)* Hello... Kensington... *(Checks the pad.)* 1-9-1-7. Sorry? Have I got what? No, I haven't got any blueprint. Are you sure you've got the right... Hello...? He just hung up.

**Chris**   "He"? Voice like Count Dracula?

**Sally**   No. I'd say more like John Wayne. Said he wanted the blueprint.

**Chris**   The blueprint? For what?

**Sally**   He didn't say. Must be a wrong number.
          *(Mrs Davies is heard off.)*

**Mrs D**   Cooee! It's just me with the tea. *(She enters with two mugs of tea on a tray.)* Here we are.

**Chris**   Thanks, Mrs D.

**Mrs D**   Are you getting yourselves organised then? *(Her tone suggests that she was expecting to see decorating in progress by now.)*

**Sally**   No, not yet. We keep getting held up by strange phone calls.

**Mrs D**   Oh. My sister in Ipswich gets those from some dirty old man.

**Sally**   Ours talks about yellow zebras and blueprints.

**Mrs D**   That's even worse. The kinky kind. *(The phone rings.)* Don't you worry. I'll sort them out for you. *(She picks up the phone.)* Now listen here you perverted person... Oh, sorry. I do beg your pardon young lady. Do you wish to speak to Mr or Mrs Taylor? No? You're calling to what...? To protest? And you're calling from where? The CND. Very nice, dear. But I don't think we want to buy anything from a catalogue today. What? No, I don't have any ballistic warheads. And even if I did, young lady, it would be no business of yours. I beg your pardon? *(She slams down the phone.)* Impudence! I'm not having some young whippersnapper making comments about my proliferating arsenal! You won't hear from her again.

**Sally**    Probably not.

**Mrs D**    Well... can't stand here chit-chatting. I'll leave you to get *on* with things. I'll come back for the cups later. Don't forget, if you need me, I'm just next door. *(She exits.)*

**Chris**    That's what's beginning to worry me.

**Sally**    We'd better "get *on* with things".

**Chris**    Yes. Let's produce some evidence before she comes back. *(He moves the ladder slightly.)* There we are.

**Sally**    Very good, Chris. But we'll need to really begin decorating somewhere.

**Chris**    I know. But where do we start?

*(The phone rings.)*

**Sally**    Here we go again. Your turn.

**Chris**    Unless it's John Wayne. *(He answers.)* Hello? What...? Could you repeat that? *(To Sally)* Dracula. *(To phone)* Look, sorry, this means nothing to me. He's leaving where now? Yes, but... hello? Hello? Gone. *(He hangs up.)* The yellow zebra is now leaving Budapesht.

**Sally**    You mean Buda*pest*?

**Chris**    No. He definitely said Buda*pesht*.

**Sally**    That yellow zebra gets around.

*(The phone rings again.)*

**Chris**    Certainly does. *(He answers.)* Yes? What? No, hold on... I think you want my wife.

**Sally**    John Wayne?

**Chris**    Yepp.

**Sally**    *(taking phone)* Howdy! No! I told you before, I don't have your blueprint. No, not even for... how much...? Twenty thousand? Is that dollars...? Hello? Hello...? *(She hangs up.)* Find those blueprints, and we're in the money.

**Chris**    Sounds like it. But what blueprints? The duke *(Pronounced "dook".)* has to be calling the wrong number.

*(The phone rings.)*

**Sally**    Yours or mine?

**Chris**    Only one way to know. *(He picks up the phone.)* Yes? What? You'll go to thirty thousand? Thanks very much. But we do not, repeat not, have your blueprints. No. We didn't promise... You're what? You're watching us right now. *(To Sally)* He's says we're under surveillance. *(He looks anxiously around while Sally goes to the window.)* Now just a minute! I'm not being threatened by... Hello? Hello?

**Sally**    I can't see anybody or anything... except Ron.

**Chris**    *(hanging up)* Is he still there?

**Sally**    Yes. Loading his van.

**Chris**    Let's get him back.

**Sally**    He might bring another "LZ" something.

**Chris**    We'll risk that to get this phone fixed.

**Sally**    OK. I'll nip down and fetch him. If that rings again, ignore it.

*(She goes out. Chris regards the phone as a menacing presence.)*

**Chris**    *(pointing at the phone.)* Don't even think about it.

*(He begins sorting out decorating items. But the phone doesn't heed his warning and rings again.)*

**Chris**    No. You're not getting me this time. *(The ringing continues.)* I can't hear you. I'm not answering. *(He holds his hands over his ears, but the phone is determined.)* Go away. *(He picks up his coat and throws it over the phone. Despite being hidden, the phone rings on regardless.)* Go away! There's nobody in! *(But he finally gives in and snatches up the phone.)* Yes...? You want a what? A visa for your cousin Vladimir in Vladivostok? No... No! Not even for a bottle of your grandmother's home-made vodka! You've got the wrong... hello?

*(With an exasperated cry, he hangs up and throws his coat over the phone. While his back is turned, a woman appears at the doorway. She looks like something out of a Greta Garbo film; fur hat, long dark coat and boots. When she speaks, her accent is equally Greta Garbo. She studies him for a moment before speaking seductively.)*

**Ludmila**    Hello darlink.

**Chris**    *(casually)* Hello... *(Turns away - then does classic double-take.)* Hello!

**Ludmila**    Hello. Are you alone, darlink?

**Chris**    Did you say "darlink"? This is flat number seven. If you're looking for Doctor Zhivago, I think you've got the wrong flat.

**Ludmila**    *(entering)* No, darlink. I think I am come to the right place.

**Chris**    Who are you? What do you want?

**Ludmila**    You can call me Ludmila. And I vant a little something you have.

**Chris** *(backing away)* Something I have?

**Ludmila** Yes, darlink. *(Moving closer.)* Don't be so coy with your typical British stiff upper collar. I think you are having it.

**Chris** *(cornered)* Having what?

**Ludmila** Just give me what I vant.

**Chris** But I don't know what you vant... want! Look, I'm a respectable married man. Only just, I'll admit. Married, I mean, not respectable. Yes, I am respectable. But not just... What am I saying?

**Ludmila** You try to pull the wool over my hat. Where is it?

**Chris** Oh... in the hall. First on the left.
*(The phone starts ringing again.).*

**Ludmila** Ah! I am hearing it!

**Chris** I wish I wasn't.

**Ludmila** I am hearing it, but I am not seeing it. *(She approaches the chair.)* Is under here. *(She whips off his coat and casts it aside.)*

**Chris** Do you mind? That cost me five guineas.

**Ludmila** I knew you have it. Now I vant it!

**Chris** You mean this is *your* phone?

**Ludmila** Da.

**Chris** Great. Then you answer it. *(He picks up the phone and thrusts it into her hands.)*

**Ludmila** Alo? Pavtariti pazhálsta? Nyet. Ya na panimáyu. *(To Chris)* I am not following. You take. *(She returns the phone.)*

**Chris** Oh, no. *(He answers)* Hello? Yes? What…? You want to order a twelve-inch what? A pepperoni pizza? Sorry, we don't do pizzas. No. Yes, you do have the wrong number. No! We don't do kebabs either! *(He hangs up and turns to Ludmila.)* Let me get this straight. Are you a neighbour we haven't met yet, and *we've* got *your* phone?

**Ludmila** Phone is mine. You give?

**Chris** I'd love to. But I don't think I'm allowed to. Not without an "LZ" something.

**Ludmila** What is "LZ"?

**Chris** Don't ask. But there's a man on the way who'll be only too happy to tell you.

**Ludmila** Coming here? Another member of your network?

**Chris** My what?

**Ludmila** I will return. Dasvydanya. *(She sweeps out.)*

**Chris** Yes, but... *(She is gone. The phone rings again)* Don't you start again! *(He answers)* What? No! We don't have your silly blueprints! I think you want to talk to our neighbour, Ludmila. Yes, Ludmila!
*(Sally returns with Ron in tow. He is minus his toolbox but is clutching his precious clipboard.)*

**Chris** Hello... hello? *(He hangs up.)*

**Sally** Lewd who?

**Chris** Thank goodness. As you were coming in, did you see a rather glamorous...? *(He stalls when he realises what he is saying.)* em...

**Sally** A glamorous what?

**Chris** Er... nothing. Forget it.

**Sally** You said "a rather glamorous"...
*(Chris is rescued by the phone.)*

**Chris** There's the phone.

**Sally** Hang on...

**Chris** *(gladly picking up the phone.)* Kensington...some number or another. Can I help you? Yes? Nice to hear from you again. *(To the others)* Dracula. *(To phone)* I was beginning to miss the good old yellow zebra. *(Ron doesn't quite know how to take this.)* Yes? Message understood. Give my regards to the rest of the herd. *(He hangs up.)*

**Sally** So? Where's the yellow zebra now?

**Chris** Arriving in Helsinki.

**Sally** That was fast.

**Ron** *(impatiently clearing his throat.)* Excuse me. I hate to disturb your psychedelic day trip, but I forgot to give you your LZ406.

**Chris** We don't need an LZ406. We need...

**Ron** I can't leave without it. Your LZ406 acknowledges delivery and installation of your apparatus.

**Sally** But as I told you downstairs, we're getting peculiar calls on our "apparatus".

**Ron** Peculiar? I see. *(He readies his clipboard.)* I'll need to know every detail...strictly for the records.

**Chris** Not *that* kind of peculiar. Just a lot of wrong numbers.

**Ron** In that case, you need an LZ622.

**Sally** No! Just fix this phone.

**Ron** Sorry, I don't fix. I only install.

**Sally**       Please? It might only be a teensy-weensy fix.

**Ron**       I can't even look at a repair engineer's work. Do you want to start a national strike? I'll tell you what I can do for you.

**Chris**       Yes?

**Ron**       Make sure you have the correct repair form. You want an LZ220.

**Chris**       *(falling to his knees)* Please, not another "LZ".

**Sally**       *(also on her knees)* We only want you to do something about this phone.

               *(The phone rings.)*

**Ron**       Ah-hah! Stand back. Leave this to me. *(He lifts the phone in an officious manner.)* Good morning. This is Kensington...er... *(He has to check his own paperwork.)* 1-9-1-7. Who is on the line? You have a call from where? From where? The Kremlin? Oh, yes... and this is number ten Downing Street. Kindly get of this line before I serve you with an LZ1000. *(He hangs up)* There. The very mention of a 1000 never fails.

               *(Chris and Sally have listened to this conversation in complete astonishment.)*

**Chris**       Do you realise who that was?

**Ron**       Yes. Just some hoaxer.

**Sally**       You've probably caused a diplomatic incident.

**Chris**       Or worse. Even as we talk, Red Army tanks could be rolling across the Berlin wall.

**Sally**       That is definitely not our phone.

**Ron**       Yes, it is. And to prove it, I've got your LZ702 here *(He checks the form.)* This is number five?

**Sally**       Yes.

**Ron**       Flat seven?

**Chris**       Definitely.

**Ron**       And this 702 is clearly signed by... *(He hesitates.)*

**Chris**       Yes?

**Ron**       *(squirming)* By a Boris Demeyenko.

**Sally**       Boris Demeyenko?

**Chris**       *(snatching Ron'S clipboard.)* Let me see that.

**Ron**       You can't look at that. You're not an authorised person.

**Chris**       *(reading)* "Boris Demeyenko. Deputy Security Attaché to the Consulate of the Union of Soviet Socialistic Republics".

**Ron**       The where?

**Chris**       The Russian Embassy, you idiot!

| | |
|---|---|
| **Ron** | Impossible. *(He snatches back his clipboard.)* This clearly says number five. |
| **Chris** | *(snatching it back again.)* Yes, it does say number five. But it also names the street, which just happens *not* to be this street. And it also says *room* seven, not *flat* seven. *(He returns the clipboard to Ron.)* |
| **Ron** | No! This isn't my fault! Look at the writing. Bad handwriting means bad paperwork. Never in ten years have I delivered a telephone to the wrong address. |
| **Sally** | You have now. We've got the Russian Embassy's phone! |
| **Ron** | Very sorry. But there's nothing I can do about it. |
| **Chris** | Yes, you can. You must have an "LZ" something for this sort of mess. |
| **Ron** | Well, I'll have a look. *(He starts hunting amongst his forms.)* |
| **Sally** | *(to Chris)* Don't encourage him. We just want rid of this phone before it rings again. |
| | *(It rings.)* |
| | Me and my big mouth. |
| **Ron** | *(about to take the call.)* I'll take this. |
| **Chris** | *(snatching the phone.)* Oh no you don't! You've already started world war three! *(Answers phone.)* Hello... can I sincerely apologise for... oh... sorry... I though you were someone else. |
| **Sally** | Dracula? |
| **Chris** | No. John Wayne. *(He hands her the phone.)* |
| **Sally** | Yes? What? No, I still haven't got your blueprints. Sorry? What? Now just a minute... Hello...? Hello? *(She hangs up.)* John Wayne says I'd better change my "toon", fast. |
| **Chris** | Your tune? |
| **Sally** | No. My "toon". |
| **Chris** | Right! That's it. We're not putting up with threats. *(He picks up the phone.)* It's time we made our first call. |
| **Sally** | Who are you calling? |
| **Chris** | It's time to get the police. |
| **Ludmila** | *(returns.)* I would not be doing that, darlink. |
| **Sally** | Who's this? And did she just call you "darling"? |
| **Ron** | No. I think she called him "darlink". |
| **Sally** | Don't you start! |
| **Chris** | *(hastily replacing the phone.)* I wasn't doing that. |
| **Ludmila** | Darlink, you were calling your secret police. |
| **Sally** | *(to Chris)* Do you know this woman? |

**Chris** No! Well... yes... no! Not personally. I know her name's Ludmila.

**Sally** You're on first name terms?

**Chris** I thought she was a neighbour.

**Sally** I see. Came in to borrow some sugar, did she?

**Chris** No! This, apparently, is her phone. Which means she must be from the Russian embassy.

**Ludmila** Da. The gentleman wins the cocktail. So you give me my phone.

*(This is not a request. She goes to take it.)*

**Ron** One moment, please. *(He picks up the phone.)* You can't hand over GPO property to an unauthorised person. *(To Ludmila)* If you are from the Russian embassy, madam, I will require valid identification.

**Ludmila** We do not carry identity card. My department is not revealing itself.

**Sally** And which department is that?

**Ludmila** The Bureau of Culture, Tourism and Sanitation.

**Chris** Which is absolutely nothing to do with security?

**Ludmila** *(laughing)* Security? Are you thinking I am some kind of secret agent? A spy?

*(Everybody laughs - with varying degrees of uncertainty.)*

You should not believe everything you are reading in *Pravda*. I am just like your British civil serving. Now give me my telephone.

**Ron** Not so fast. First, you'll need to complete an LZ260. *(He selects the necessary form from his clipboard.)*

**Ludmila** What is the LZ260?

**Chris/Sally** Don't ask!

**Ron** This, madam, is the official GPO form for the re-direction of incorrectly delivered equipment. Don't forget to complete both sides and sign here... here... and date and sign here.

**Ludmila** You call that bourgeois capitalist scrap an official form? At Moscow Central, you vant a pencil, you have the ten page form... in triplicate!

**Ron** *(genuinely impressed)* Wow!

**Chris** Moscow Central?

**Ludmila** Bureau of Culture, Tourism...

**Chris/Sally** And Sanitation.

**Ron** My LZ260 may only be a humble two pages, but it must be completed. If you please?

**Ludmila** No time! I take phone now.

**Ron** *(picking up the phone and hugging it protectively.)* No LZ260, no phone. And nothing will change my mind.

**Ludmila** No, comrade? *(She reaches into her coat pocket and pulls out a pistol.)* Not even this? *(She points the pistol at him.)*

**Ron** *(not taking this in)* Now, madam, I do have the proper form for making a complaint... *(It suddenly dawns on him.)* That's a gun!

**Chris** Of course it's a gun, you idiot! And it's pointed at us! *(To Ludmila)* What are you doing with that?

**Sally** Yes! Why does a civil serving... servant... need a gun?

**Ludmila** It is dangerous work at the Bureau.

**Sally** Of Culture and Tourism?

**Chris/Ron** And Sanitation.

**Ludmila** It is my duty to protect the property of the Soviet Union.

**Ron** This is Post Office property; and until it's signed for, nothing will make me let go of this phone.

*(It rings. Everybody jumps- especially Ron, who hastily puts it down.)*

**Ludmila** *(to Chris)* You answer.

**Chris** You answer! It's your phone. It might be a cultured tourist complaining about their hotel loo.

*(She picks up the phone, but doesn't answer at first.)*

But it's more likely to be John Wayne or the pink giraffe.

*(She reacts by immediately hanging up.)*

**Ludmila** *(dramatically:)* You know about the pink giraffe?

**Chris** No! No! I was kidding.

**Ludmila** You know too much, darlink. You will have to be silenced.

**Chris** I'm not going to say another word.

**Ludmila** *(taking the safety catch off the pistol.)* Sorry, darlink. *(She aims at him.)* I am meaning the permanent silence. But first, tell me who you vork for?

**Chris** The Westminster Bank.

**Ludmila** No, darlink. I vant to know who you *really* vork for? M.I.5? The C.I.A.?

**Sally** Now look here...

*(Ludmila turns the pistol on Sally.)*

**Chris** Will you stop waving that thing about! If that goes off, it'll be like Emergency Ward Ten in here.

**Ludmila** You are all operatives in this western spy ring I am infiltrating. For this achievement, I will be rewarded by mother Russia! The Order of Lenin!

**Ron** I don't care who's giving your orders. All this is nothing to do with me. So I'll just be off.
*(He makes a move towards the door, but finds Ludmila and her pistol blocking his way.)*

**Ludmila** Halt, comrade. You think I let one of the ringleaders jump the nest like the sinking rat?

**Ron** Ringleader? I'm just a telephone engineer!

**Ludmila** A telephone engineer? Hah! You are obviously the electronic surveillance brains of this spy ring.

**Chris** Now that is being ridiculous.

**Sally** Calling him the "brains".

**Ludmila** Nobody will leave here.

**Chris** I'm not arguing. But how did you know *your* phone was in *our* flat?

**Ludmila** Simple, darlink. We are tapping the line. How you say, the bug?

**Chris** I see. *(He thinks)* But how did you happen to have *this* line tapped? *(Thinks more.)* You mean you've got *every* phone line in London tapped?

**Ludmila** Now you know even more too much. I regret you must all be eliminated. *(Raises her pistol.)* State secrets must be kept.

**Ron** What sort of secrets does the Bureau of Culture and Tourism....?

**Chris/Sally/Ludmila** And Sanitation!

**Ron** And Sanitation have?

**Ludmila** Ah. That would be telling secrets.

**Chris** I think we're in trouble.

**Ron** Big trouble. The first time in my life I've been in this dilemma, and I haven't got one.

**Sally** Got what?

**Ron** An LZ900.

**Chris** Why the hell do you want an LZ900?

**Ron** Sudden death of an employee while on GPO business.

**Chris** You're worried about a silly form at a time like this?
*(The phone rings. Chris snatches it.)*

**Chris** Hello! Yes? What...? What...? Wrong number? What do you mean, "wrong number"?

| | |
|---|---|
| **Sally** | *(nudging Chris and whispering.)* 999! |
| **Chris** | You should be John Wayne, or Dracula or the zebra from Vladivostok. *(Responding to Sally'S nudges.)* What? |
| **Sally** | Get them to call 999! |
| **Chris** | Yes! *(to phone)* Hello! Sorry! Sorry! Didn't mean to shout. Could you please call the Police? Yes, the Police! We need the Police... now! |
| | *(At that precise moment, P.C. Nash enters, followed by Mrs Davies.)* |
| **Nash** | What's going on here then? |
| **Chris** | Wow! That's amazing! *(To phone)* I don't know you did that, but thanks! *(He hangs up.)* |
| **Sally** | Fab! *(To Ludmila)* I'll bet your Moscow Police couldn't beat that. |
| **Ron** | You can always depend on a London bobby. |
| **Ludmila** | *(flourishing her pistol)* Stay back! I am armed and hazardous! |
| **Mrs D** | *(to Nash)* There. I told you something funny was going on in here, didn't I? I did hear somebody shouting about a gun. *(To the others)* I practically had to drag this officer from the street. *(To Nash)* Didn't believe me, did you? |
| **Nash** | Yes, madam. Thank you, madam. Leave this to me. |
| **Ludmila** | Keep the distance! I give you the varnink! |
| **Nash** | Don't you mean "warning"? |
| **Mrs D** | No. I think she said "varnink". |
| **Ron** | No. Sounded more like "varnish". |
| **Nash** | Please? *(To Ludmila)* Now then, madam. Do you think you're in a James Bond film? I'll take this, thank you. *(Nash calmly takes the pistol.)* Have you any idea how dangerous these things are? |
| **Mrs D** | Not to mention noisy. |
| **Nash** | Not to mention... *(To Mrs D)* Please, madam? |
| | *(The phone rings. This shocks Ludmila out of her surprised stupor. With a loud shout, she jumps into a "kung fu" stance. She throws an arm forward, but Nash catches her wrist and slips on handcuffs. Ludmila tries a jab with her other arm, but Nash simply repeats the process. Ludmila is now handcuffed by both wrists.)* |
| **Ludmila** | I protest! I claim diplomatic immunization! |
| **Nash** | Whatever you say, madam. You can explain all that to the desk sergeant. Will someone please answer that phone? |
| | *(But nobody does.)* |

**Mrs D**    That's what I was telling you. This nice young couple have had nothing but strange calls.

**Nash**    I understand. Let me deal with this. *(Picks up the phone.)* Hello? Yes? Who is calling? The Kremlin? Oh, yes. Very funny. And I'm Sherlock Holmes. *(Or Miss Marple.)* Please get off the line. You're hindering a Police investigation. *(Hangs up.)*

**Sally**    Then this woman, who's some kind of spy from the Russian embassy, demanded our phone at gun point.

**Nash**    I see. Messy business. So who is responsible for this telephone?

*(Chris, Sally, Mrs D and Ludmila point at Ron.)*

**Ron**    Me? I was only doing my job.

**Nash**    And you are, sir?

**Ron**    Ron. GPO telephone engineer.

**Nash**    Right. First things first. We don't want any more comedians on the line. Can you get this line disconnected at the exchange?

**Ron**    Can do, but... *(He searches for the inevitable "LZ".)* that will require a completed LZ844.

**Nash**    What's an LZ844?

**Chris/Sally/Mrs D/Ludmila** Don't ask!

**Ron**    Authorisation to disconnect. *(Hands it to Nash.)* Don't forget to complete both sides, and sign here... here... and date and sign here.

**Nash**    Sorry, sir. We don't have time for this nonsense.

**Ron**    Nonsense? This is an official GPO form. Well. I'm sorry too. No LZ844. No disconnection.

**Nash**    You'd rather be arrested for obstructing a Police investigation?

**Ron**    *(picking up the phone and dialling.)* I'll get it disconnected right away, officer. *(Takes the phone a distance and talks quietly to the exchange.)*

**Ludmila** My government will be protesting at your highest level! Throw me into your darkest cell! Give me the three degrees! But I will never expose myself. Never!

**Ron**    *(hangs up and puts the phone back on the chair.)* That's it disconnected.

**Chris**    It's not that I don't believe you... *(He picks up the phone.)* But... *(He checks.)*

**Sally**    Well?

**Chris**    *(hanging up)* No dialling tone. Completely dead.

**Nash**    Good. That phone is obviously a vital piece of evidence. We'll need it down at the station.

**Ron**    You can't do that. Not without an LZ607.

**Nash**    No, I'm not going to ask.

**Ron**    Requisition of GPO property for a criminal investigation. *(He hands it to Nash.)* Don't forget to complete...

**Nash**    Look, sir, do you know how much time we waste at the station filling out idiotic forms instead of nicking villains like Mata Hari here? I'll deal with this later. Right now, you'll all have to accompany me to the station.
*(Protests all round - especially from Ron.)*

**Ron**    I'm going nowhere until I've had my paperwork. I've not had one completed LZ since I came here. *(to Chris)* You never did complete your 406 acknowledging delivery. *(He hands it to Chris and then turns to Nash.)* And I'm still waiting for your 844 and your 607. And I'll also need an LZ750. *(Nash is given a third form.)* Unauthorised absence from GPO duty. Well?
*(Chris and Nash consider their respective forms.)*

**Chris**    You want me to sign for a phone that was never mine and is about to be taken away? *(He crushes the form and throws it away.)* There! Is that complete enough for you?

**Ron**    You've just destroyed an LZ406! Never, in ten years in this job, has anybody dared to touch an LZ406! Right! *(He pulls out another form.)* You asked for this! An LZ500! Vandalism of GPO property. *(He presents it to Nash.)* Your department I think.

**Chris**    *(To Nash)* Don't forget to complete inside-out and upside-down. And sign here, there, and everywhere.

**Nash**    *(to Ron)* Certainly, sir. I'll deal with this right away. *(Crushes the form and throws it away.)*

**Ron**    You've just vandalised my vandalism form!

**Sally**    Bet you don't have an LZ for that.

**Nash**    I really need some assistance here.

**Mrs D**    With pleasure. *(Takes a form from Nash.)* May I?

**Nash**    Please do.
*(Mrs Davies gleefully destroys another form.)*

**Ron**    You can't do that!

**Chris**    Watch us!
*(Nash has two forms left. Chris destroys one. Nash destroys the other.)*

**Nash**    That was easy.

**Chris**    That was fun. *(He grabs Ron'S clipboard.)* Let's complete all the rest!

*(They soon empty the clipboard in a form trashing frenzy. Crushed forms are tossed in the air, at each other, and at Ron. His expression is one of a man whose worst possible nightmare is happening right in front of him. Meanwhile, Ludmila realises she has been temporarily forgotten and edges towards the door. When she reaches the door, she beckons Ron with a "this way" gesture. He is only too glad to an escape, and they both make a hasty departure. The paperwork orgy ends with all four exhilarated and out of breath.)*

**Chris**    That was the best bit of paperwork I've ever done.

**Nash**    I'd love to do that down at the station. Which reminds me... It's time I was... *(Looks round to find no Ludmila.)* Hello, where's she gone?

**Sally**    Looks like Olga from the Volga's done a runner.

**Chris**    With Ron!

**Nash**    And she's got my best pair of handcuffs! Oh, no! The sergeant'll have me scrubbing out the cells for this.

*(Nash rushes out in pursuit. Sally has gone to the window.)*

**Sally**    There they go... In Ron's van!

**Mrs D**    What a carry on! If this is what happens when you get your own phone, I'm glad I use a call box. I'd better get back. Ralph will be wondering where I've got to. I left him panting on the bed.

**Chris**    Oh, yes?

**Sally**    *(giving him a nudge.)* Ralph's her dog.

**Chris**    Oh, right. 'Bye, Mrs D.

*(Mrs Davies exits.)*

**Chris**    That's better. Just the two of us.

**Sally**    *(glancing anxiously at the phone.)* Not quite.

**Chris**    *(picks up the phone and listens.)* Don't worry. Dead line. *(He hangs up.)*

**Sally**    So, what now?

**Chris**    *(picking up rolls of paper.)* There's only one thing for it.

**Sally**    You're right. Why not? *(She picks up brushes and paste.)* But where on earth do we start?

**Chris**    *(looking at the "fourth" wall.)* Why don't we start with this one? *(They both face the chosen wall, their arms filled with decorating items. There is a brief pause before their return to normality is shattered by the ringing of the phone. They look at the phone is dismay, drop everything on the floor, grab their coats, and flee the room. As the phone continues to ring...)*

**Curtain**

## Author's Note
Any resemblance between Ron's forms and real G.P.O. paperwork of the period is purely accidental (I hope!)

## Furniture & Property List

*On Stage*    One chair
Stepladder
Tins of paint
Radio
Toolbox
Red telephone *(in cardboard box)*

*Off Stage*    Two mugs of tea on a tray *(Mrs Davies)*

*Personal*    Newspaper *(Ron)*
Mug or cup *(Ron)*
Clipboard with numerous forms *(Ron)*
Tins of Paint *(Chris)*
Wallpaper. *(Sally)*
Handbag or shoulder bag containing notepad & pen *(Sally)*
Gun* *(Ludmila)*
Handcuffs *(P.C. Nash)*

*Please remember to check if any regulations for use apply

## Lighting Plot
*Practical fittings required* none
*To open*    General interior lighting (No changes required)

## Effects Plot
*To open*    *Opening music – The James Bond theme.*

## Other Plays by Alan Richardson
Mr Perfect
The Spy Who Came in for the Phone
When A Man Knows
The Worst Day of My Life

www.ingramcontent.com/pod-product-compliance
Lightning Source LLC
Chambersburg PA
CBHW060606030426
42337CB00019B/3634